THE GREAT BIBLE

DISCOVERY

THE LIFE AND WORK OF JESUS

THE BIBLE IS A BEST-SELLER. IT IS ALSO ONE OF THE MASTER-WORKS OF WORLD LITERATURE - SO IMPORTANT THAT UNIVERSITIES TODAY TEACH 'NON-RELIGIOUS' BIBLE COURSES TO HELP STUDENTS WHO CHOOSE TO STUDY WESTERN LITERATURE.

THE BIBLE POSSESSES AN AMAZING POWER TO FASCINATE YOUNG AND OLD ALIKE.

ONE REASON FOR THIS UNIVERSAL APPEAL IS THAT IT DEALS WITH BASIC HUMAN LONGINGS, EMOTIONS, RELATIONSHIPS. 'ALL THE WORLD IS HERE.' ANOTHER REASON IS THAT SO MUCH OF THE BIBLE CONSISTS OF STORIES. THEY ARE FULL OF MEANING BUT EASY TO REMEMBER.

HERE ARE THOSE STORIES, PRESENTED SIMPLY AND WITH A MINIMUM OF EXPLANATION. WE HAVE LEFT THE TEXT TO SPEAK FOR ITSELF. GIFTED ARTISTS USE THE ACTION-STRIP TECHNIQUE TO BRING THE BIBLE'S DEEP MESSAGE TO READERS OF ALL AGES. THEIR DRAWINGS ARE BASED ON INFORMATION FROM ARCHAEOLOGICAL DISCOVERIES COVERING FIFTEEN CENTURIES.

AN ANCIENT BOOK - PRESENTED FOR THE PEOPLE OF THE SECOND MILLENNIUM. A RELIGIOUS BOOK - PRESENTED FREE FROM THE INTERPRETATION OF ANY PARTICULAR CHURCH. A UNIVERSAL BOOK - PRESENTED IN A FORM THAT ALL MAY ENJOY.

M publishing
CARLISLE, UK

20

After being baptized by his cousin John, Jesus began his public ministry. His words and actions challenged people to respond to the Kingdom of God which was already present among them.

Although he received no formal training, Jesus was often addressed as rabbi (= teacher). The same title was given to recognized teachers among the Pharisees. Like other rabbis, he attracted students ('disciples') who learned from him. He chose twelve of these as apostles (or special representatives). Just as twelve tribes had formed the nation of Israel, the people of God under the Old Covenant, so these twelve would be the beginning of a new people of God.

Jesus lived a simple life. During his public ministry he depended on what people gave him. He mixed with those who were generally regarded as sinners. He spent much time in prayer. Like the prophets of old, he spoke in public. Like them too he challenged many of the religious ideas of his day. He spoke of God's love and forgiveness but warned of his judgement. Although he accepted the title 'prophet', he did not like to be called 'messiah', possibly because the title had warlike overtones. From boyhood he knew that God was his Father in a special way and occasionally spoke of himself as 'the Son (of God)'. He often spoke of himself as the Son of Man - referring to a mysterious figure associated in the Book of Daniel and with the coming of the Kingdom of God.

The religious leaders were hostile to Jesus. He spoke as if God were his own father. He said that when the End came, people would be judged by him and by the way they had responded to him. He claimed authority to forgive sins. Although his moral code was strict, he rejected many of the religious traditions which were very important to them.

At first Jesus attracted large crowds. His personality, teaching and acts of mercy had a wide appeal. Later he came to be seen as a more controversial figure and in Jerusalem he was opposed both by the Pharisees and the temple authorities.

MATTHEW 5:14-18:20
MARK 4-9
LUKE 3; 7; 9-13; 18
JOHN 4; 6

THE LIFE AND WORK OF JESUS

First published as *Découvrir la Bible* 1983

First edition © Librairie Larousse 1983
English translation © Daan Retief Publishers 1990
24-volume series adaptation by Mike Jacklin © Knowledge Unlimited 1994
This edition © OM Publishing 1995

01 00 99 98 97 96 95   7 6 5 4 3 2 1

OM Publishing is an imprint of Send the Light Ltd.,
P.O. Box 300, Carlisle, Cumbria CA3 0QS, U.K.

Series editor: D. Roy Briggs
English translation: Bethan Uden
Introductions: Peter Cousins

British Library Cataloguing in Publication Data
A catalogue record for this book is available from the British Library
ISBN 1-85078-224-5

Printed in Singapore by Tien Wah Press (Pte) Ltd.

JESUS
AND THE TWELVE

TRAVELLING THROUGHOUT GALILEE, JESUS OF NAZARETH, ACCOMPANIED BY THE TWELVE APOSTLES CONTINUES TO WORK WONDERS AND MIRACLES... EVEN THOUGH THE SCRIBES AND THE PHARISEES ARE AGAINST HIM.

HE'S JUST DELIVERED MY SON OF AN EVIL SPIRIT!

HARDLY SURPRISING! HE HIMSELF SERVES THE PRINCE OF DEVILS!

SCENARIO: Etienne DAHLER
DRAWING: José BIELSA

A COUNTRY AT WAR WITH ITSELF WILL BE DESTROYED. IF SATAN'S FIGHTING AGAINST HIMSELF, HOW CAN HE CONTINUE TO LIVE?

HE'S RIGHT! YOUR ACCUSATIONS DON'T MAKE SENSE!

EITHER THAT MAN COMES FROM GOD, OR HE'S SENT BY SATAN...

YOU STILL DARE TO ASK THAT QUESTION AFTER WHAT YOU'VE JUST SEEN?

3

5

A LITTLE LATER...

RABBI, NOT ALL OF US UNDERSTOOD YOUR PARABLE...

YET IT'S QUITE SIMPLE: THE SOWER SOWS GOD'S WORD...

... SOME HEAR IT, BUT THEN SATAN COMES AND SNATCHES IT AWAY...

LIKE THE SCRIBES AND THE PHARISEES THE OTHER DAY!

...OTHERS DON'T LET IT TAKE ROOT, SO THEY DON'T LAST LONG. WHEN THE FIRST TEST COMES, THEY GIVE UP.

... IN OTHERS THEIR WORRIES AND DESIRES CHOKE THE WORD.

BUT EVERYONE HAS SOME GOOD SOIL.

YOU'RE RIGHT, JOHN, BUT THIS GROUND NEEDS TO BE WORKED...

WHY WERE YOU FRIGHTENED? DO YOU STILL HAVE NO FAITH?

WHO IS THIS MAN? EVEN THE WIND AND THE SEA OBEY HIM!

AFTER A FEW DAYS IN THE LAND OF THE GADARENES,* JESUS CROSSED BACK TO CAPERNAUM.

* People of Gadara, south-east of Lake Tiberias.

A LARGE CROWD WAS ALREADY WAITING FOR HIM.

RABBI, MY DAUGHTER'S DYING! COME AND LAY YOUR HANDS ON HER, AND SAVE HER LIFE!

JAIRUS, TAKE ME TO HER.

JAIRUS IS AN OFFICIAL IN THE SYNAGOGUE IN CAPERNAUM.

JESUS! HEAL ME!

HAVE PITY, MASTER!

IF I COULD JUST TOUCH HIS CLOAK, I'M SURE I'D BE CURED.

THERE WAS ALSO A WOMAN WHO HAD BEEN BLEEDING BADLY FOR 12 YEARS...

WHY ALL THIS NOISE? THE LITTLE ONE'S NOT DEAD; SHE'S ONLY ASLEEP.

WE'RE SURE SHE'S DEAD! YOU CAN'T DO ANYTHING MORE FOR HER, JESUS!

IT'S ALL OVER! HER BODY'S ALREADY GETTING COLD.

LITTLE ONE, I TELL YOU TO GET UP!

MY CHILD!

DON'T TELL ANYONE WHAT HAPPENED.

BUT THE NEWS SOON SPREAD THROUGH THE WHOLE REGION.

A LITTLE LATER...

IT'S HE! IT'S JESUS OF NAZARETH!

YOU SEE, PETER? THE SMALLEST VILLAGE WELCOMES ME... AND MY OWN PEOPLE REJECT ME... BUT I CAN'T ABANDON THEM... LET'S GO BACK TO NAZARETH!

11

ON THE SABBATH JESUS WENT TO THE SYNAGOGUE IN NAZARETH. HE'D ATTENDED IT FOR NEARLY 30 YEARS, SO HE KNEW IT WELL.

THE LAW OF MOSES TEACHES THAT ANYONE COMMITTING A CRIME MUST BE PUNISHED BY THE JUDGES...

...BUT I SAY TO YOU: WHOEVER IS ANGRY WITH HIS BROTHER, DESERVES PUNISHMENT JUST AS MUCH.

YOU'VE COME TO GIVE US A LESSON, YOU WORKER OF MIRACLES?

YOU CAN SEE HE'S GONE MAD!

ANYONE WHO CALLS HIS BROTHER A FOOL, DESERVES TO BE THROWN INTO THE FIRE OF GEHENNA!

SILENCE!

JESUS, YOU'RE ONE OF US... BUT YOU MUST UNDERSTAND THAT WE CAN'T ACCEPT WHAT YOU'RE SUGGESTING.

I TELL YOU THE TRUTH. A PROPHET'S REJECTED ONLY IN HIS OWN LAND.

THEN JESUS AND THE TWELVE LEFT NAZARETH.

HOW CAN PEOPLE BE SO STUBBORN?

MASTER, IF THESE PEOPLE DON'T WANT THE KINGDOM OF GOD, TELL OTHERS ABOUT IT...

YES, JOHN, THERE'S A HUGE HARVEST, BUT THERE ARE FEW WORKERS!

ONE DAY THE DISCIPLES OF JOHN THE BAPTIST CAME TO FIND JESUS.

MASTER, WE'VE TERRIBLE NEWS FOR YOU. **JOHN'S DEAD!**

HEROD ANTIPAS HAD HIM EXECUTED.

EXECUTED? HOW CAN THAT BE?

IT'S INCREDIBLE! HEROD WAS GIVING A PARTY FOR HIS BIRTHDAY...

HERODIAS, THE WIFE HE'D TAKEN FROM HIS BROTHER PHILIP, WAS THERE.

DURING THE EVENING SHE MADE HER DAUGHTER SALOME DANCE FOR THE GUESTS.

14

THEN...

YOU'VE DANCED SUPERBLY. I'LL GIVE YOU ANYTHING YOU WANT!

SALOME WENT OUT FOR A FEW MOMENTS TO ASK HER MOTHER ...

WHEN SHE CAME BACK...

I WANT THE HEAD OF JOHN THE BAPTIST ON A DISH!

WHAT?

WHAT ARE YOU SAYING?

HERODIAS HAD NEVER FORGIVEN JOHN THE BAPTIST FOR PUBLICLY CONDEMNING HER ADULTERY.

HEROD WAS CAUGHT IN A TRAP.

VERY WELL, THEN...

JOHN WAS MORE THAN A PROPHET. IT WAS HE OF WHOM IT WAS WRITTEN: I WILL SEND MY MESSENGER TO PREPARE THE WAY FOR ME.*

* Malachi 3:1

I TELL YOU, AMONG ALL HUMAN BEINGS THERE'S NO ONE GREATER THAN JOHN.

WEEKS WENT BY. SPRING WAS ALREADY COVERING THE HILLS OF GALILEE WHEN THE DISCIPLES RETURNED FROM THEIR MISSION.

MASTER, IT'S WONDERFUL TO SEE YOU AGAIN!

WELL?

WHEREVER WE WENT, MANY TURNED BACK TO GOD, AND THE SICK WERE HEALED!

SOON ALL THE TWELVE WERE BACK, AND TOLD THEIR STORIES...

BUT SOMETIMES THEY CHASED US AWAY...

AND NOW WHAT ARE WE GOING TO DO? CAN WE ALWAYS LIVE BY BEGGING OUR BREAD, WITHOUT EVEN KNOWING IN THE MORNING WHERE WE'LL SLEEP THAT NIGHT?

HE'S RIGHT. WE HAVE FAMILIES, CHILDREN... WE MUST SEE TO THEIR NEEDS.

THE BIRDS OF THE SKY DON'T SOW OR REAP, BUT GOD FEEDS THEM...

18

MEANWHILE, PETER ON HIS SHIP, IN THE MIDDLE OF THE NIGHT...

THE WIND'S AGAINST US!

WELL, ROW HARDER THEN!

SUDDENLY...

AAAAH!! A GHOST!

BUT PETER, YOU AREN'T GOING TO...

COME!

CHEER UP! IT'S I. DON'T BE AFRAID.

MASTER, IF IT REALLY IS YOU, ORDER ME TO COME TO YOU.

... WALK ON THE WATER!

I'M FRIGHTENED!

THE NEXT DAY THE CROWD SET OFF TO LOOK FOR JESUS.

A LITTLE LATER, IN THE SYNAGOGUE IN CAPERNAUM, WHERE MANY WERE TURNING AGAINST JESUS...

YOUR FATHERS ATE MANNA IN THE DESERT AND THEY DIED. BUT THOSE WHO EAT THE BREAD OF HEAVEN WILL LIVE FOR EVER.

AND THIS BREAD IS MY FLESH WHICH I GIVE FOR THE LIFE OF THE WORLD.

HOW CAN HE GIVE US HIS FLESH TO EAT?

THOSE WHO EAT MY FLESH AND DRINK MY BLOOD HAVE ETERNAL LIFE. I WILL RAISE THEM UP TO LIFE ON THE LAST DAY.

THAT'S TOO MUCH!

OUTSIDE THE SYNAGOGUE THE DISCIPLES TRIED TO WORK THIS OUT...

IT'S VERY DIFFICULT! HOW CAN WE UNDERSTAND IT?

AND HOW CAN HE SAY THAT?

THE WORDS I'VE SPOKEN TO YOU ARE SPIRIT AND LIFE. BUT THERE ARE MANY AMONG YOU WHO DON'T BELIEVE IT!

JESUS

AMONG THE PAGANS

SCENARIO : Etienne DAHLER
DRAWING: Pierre FRISANO

THE WHOLE COUNTRY SOON HEARD ABOUT JESUS.

LITTLE ONE, I WANT YOU TO BE HEALED!

THAT NIGHT...

JESUS, MANY OF THESE PEOPLE WANT TO FOLLOW US...

WELL AND GOOD! LET THEM COME WITH US!

BUT... THEY'RE NOT JEWS!

JAMES, THE KINGDOM IS FOR THEM ALSO!

DIDN'T THE PROPHET ISAIAH SAY: YOU WILL CALL THE NATIONS WHOM YOU DO NOT KNOW AND THEY WILL RUN TO YOU, BECAUSE OF THE LORD YOUR GOD?

IT'S TIME TO GET A LITTLE REST. TOMORROW WE'LL MOVE EASTWARDS.

DON'T BE AFRAID, LITTLE FLOCK... YOUR FATHER'S SEEN FIT TO GIVE YOU THE KINGDOM.

THE NEXT DAY JESUS AND HIS DISCIPLES SET OFF INTO THE INTERIOR OF THE COUNTRY.

WE'LL CROSS THAT MOUNTAIN.

LOOK! A CARAVAN OF CAMELS!

THE KINGDOM'S LIKE THIS. THE ROAD TO DESTRUCTION IS WIDE, WITH PLENTY OF ROOM, AND THAT'S WHY MANY TAKE IT...

...BUT THE ROAD TO LIFE IS STEEP AND DIFFICULT... FEW PEOPLE FIND THAT ROAD!

THE LITTLE GROUP CONTINUED ON THEIR WAY, BUT SUDDENLY...

JESUS, WE CAN'T GET THROUGH!

GOING DOWN THE SYRIAN SIDE, JESUS AND HIS DISCIPLES PASSED THROUGH A VERY FERTILE AREA.

IT'S TIME TO GO BACK TO GALILEE.

IN ONE VILLAGE...

MASTER, THEY TOLD US YOU COULD DO SOMETHING FOR THIS MAN.

HE'S DEAF, AND CAN HARDLY SPEAK.

JESUS TOOK HIM ON ONE SIDE...

THEN TOUCHED HIS TONGUE...

EPHPHATHA!*

THE GOD OF ISRAEL LIVES!

* Open up!

HE'S HEALED ME!

I CAN H...

AND THERE'S NO LIMIT TO H... POWER!

AFTER A BRIEF STAY BESIDE LAKE TIBERIAS, THE LITTLE GROUP WENT BACK UP THE JORDAN VALLEY TOWARDS **CAESAREA PHILIPPI**.

LOOK THERE! ANOTHER PAGAN TEMPLE!

YOU'LL SEE PLENTY MORE WHEN WE REACH PANEAS*

*'Temple of Pan', later called Banias.

AT ONE OF THE SOURCES OF THE JORDAN...

THIS IS WHERE PAGANS CELEBRATE THE WAY LIFE SPRINGS UP...

...AND END UP WORSHIPPING THIS RIVER!

AS IF WATER COULD BE GOD!

AND ME: WHO DO PEOPLE SAY THAT I AM?

SOME SAY YOU'RE JOHN THE BAPTIST.

OTHERS THAT YOU'RE ELIJAH.

I'VE HEARD THEM SAYING THAT YOU'RE THE PROPHET JEREMIAH!

BUT YOU, WHO DO YOU SAY I AM?

YOU'RE THE CHRIST,* THE SON OF THE LIVING GOD.

YOU'RE BLESSED, SIMON! MY FATHER REVEALED THIS TO YOU, NOT YOUR OWN THOUGHTS.

*The Messiah, that is, God's Anointed.

SPIRIT OF DARKNESS, I ORDER YOU TO COME OUT OF THIS BOY, AND NEVER ENTER HIM AGAIN!

HE'S DEAD!

MY SON! MY ONLY CHILD!

NOW GET UP.

JESUS, YOU'VE CURED HIM!

WHEN THE CROWD HAD GONE...

WHY COULDN'T WE DRIVE OUT THAT SPIRIT?

BECAUSE OF YOUR LACK OF FAITH... IF YOU HAD FAITH ONLY AS BIG AS A MUSTARD SEED...

...YOU COULD SAY TO THIS MOUNTAIN, 'MOVE FROM HERE TO THERE...' AND IT WOULD MOVE.

THEY LEFT THAT PLACE AND CROSSED GALILEE ON THE WAY BACK TO CAPERNAUM

I SAY PETER'S THE GREATEST AMONG US.

YOU'RE FORGETTING JOHN. JESUS LOVES HIM DEARLY.

NO, I THINK ANDREW'S THE GREATEST. HE WAS THE FIRST TO FOLLOW THE MASTER, AND BEFORE THAT HE WAS JOHN THE BAPTIST'S DISCIPLE.

AT THE END OF THEIR JOURNEY, IN PETER'S HOUSE...

WHAT WERE YOU TALKING ABOUT ON THE ROAD?

IF ONE OF YOU WANTS TO BE FIRST, LET HIM BE THE LAST, THE SERVANT OF ALL.

THE DISCIPLES WERE QUIET.

SAMUEL, COME HERE.

TRULY, I TELL YOU, UNLESS YOU BECOME LIKE LITTLE CHILDREN, YOU WILL NEVER ENTER THE KINGDOM OF HEAVEN.

41

ONE DAY, AT SYCHAR, NOT FAR FROM THE ANCIENT SHECHEM, JESUS WAS RESTING BESIDE JACOB'S WELL. THE DISCIPLES HAD GONE TO BUY FOOD.

GIVE ME A DRINK OF WATER.

WHAT? YOU, A JEW, ASKING A SAMARITAN FOR A DRINK?

IF ONLY YOU KNEW WHAT GOD GIVES! IT WOULD BE YOU WHO BEGGED ME TO GIVE YOU THE WATER OF LIFE.

BUT YOU'VE NO BUCKET. WHERE WOULD YOU GET THAT WATER?

WHOEVER DRINKS THIS WATER, WILL BE THIRSTY AGAIN, BUT ANYONE DRINKING THE WATER I GIVE, WILL NEVER BE THIRSTY AGAIN.

SIR, GIVE ME THAT WATER SO I WON'T GET THIRSTY AGAIN. THEN I WON'T HAVE TO COME HERE ANYMORE!

GO AND CALL YOUR HUSBAND; THEN COME BACK!

I HAVE NO HUSBAND!